WHY ARE YOU HERE?

WHY ARE YOU HERE?

From Chaos To Cohesion

Gloria Taylor-Boyce

Library of Congress Control Number: 2007909233
ISBN: Hardcover   978-1-4363-0493-1
                   Softcover   978-1-4363-0492-4

This book was printed in the United States of America.

To order additional copies of this book, contact:
Xlibris Corporation
1-888-795-4274
www.Xlibris.com
Orders@Xlibris.com
44451

CONTENTS

DEDICATION

To my mentor, Bishop E. Bernard Jordan, for ministering prophetically into my life and speaking the creation of this book into my ear. To Pastor Debra Jordan and the Company of Prophets, who reiterated the words of the Master Prophet; my husband, Ralph Henderson Boyce; my son, Jason Taylor; my sisters Yvonne, Annette, Claudette, Ann, Andrea, whose support strengthen me through the developmental process. Last but not least, to my lunchroom sisters. I thank you all. God bless.

THE BOOK OF HEBREWS

Prayer from the Bible

God, who at sundry times and in divers manners spake in time past unto the fathers by the prophets, Hath in these last days spoken unto us by his Son, whom he hath appointed heir of all things, by whom also he made the worlds; Who being the brightness of his glory, and the express image of his person, and upholding all things by the word of his power, when he had by himself purged our sins, sat down on the right hand of the Majesty on high: Being made so much better than the angels, as he hath by inheritance obtained a more excellent name than they. (Hebrews 1:1-4)

In these verses, the book of Hebrews is showing us that God has revealed Himself through various means, such as visions, dreams, and prophets. Christ's person, power, and position are all expressed in these verses. These verses are also saying that Jesus Christ did not become deity; He always was equal with the Father.

PREFACE

Who are you? This question is one that everyone needs to ask themselves. When I ask, who are you? I am not referring to what you are called. I am not referring to your birth name, nationality, country of origin, profession, or the fact that you are a parent. I am asking about that person inside of you. While this may seem like a simple question, many people struggle with a response. This question is difficult because we tend to identify with our chosen profession. For example, if I were to pose this question to my brother in law, he would say, "I am Dr.," and then give his name. My sister might say I am a principal and name the school. However, who are they? Very few of us take time out to ponder this age-old question. Nonetheless, if we are to succeed in life, obtain joy, happiness, and peace of mind, we must know the answer to the question, who are you?

This Question Is Difficult

Knowing the answer to who you are then conjures up another question: why are you here? We live on this vast planet called Earth with global communications and instant messaging, yet we are challenged by this question. This question is more difficult to answer and as such may pose some difficulty in our fully grasping the understanding of why we are here. In a miniquestionnaire I conducted at my place of employment, many people were honest in their responses to these questions.

THE BOOK OF HEBREWS

Prayer from the Bible

For unto which of the angels said he at any time, Thou art my Son, this day have I begotten thee? And again, I will be to him a Father, and he shall be to me a Son? And again, when he bringeth in the first begotten into the world, he saith, And let all the angels of God worship him. And of the angels he saith, Who maketh his angels spirits, and his ministers a flame of fire. But unto the Son he saith, Thy throne, O God, is for ever and ever: a sceptre of righteousness is the sceptre of thy kingdom. (Hebrews 1:5-8)

Angels are created spiritual beings who are servants of God. The word "angel" means messenger.

They often claimed, "I don't know," and some said, "To look after my children" or "To serve my country." Some identified with the importance of their job and work. While these responses are admirable and may appear factual to the world, it still begs the question, why are you here on this planet Earth? For what purpose are you here? What are you supposed to achieve? What is your purpose in life?

Achieving Simplicity

It is the writer's desire to bring simplicity to these questions. This book, while attempting to convey clarity of purpose, will help in guiding those seeking answers to these questions. The goal or aim is to take a survey of our present position with an honest view by answering these questions. This is a more difficult thing to accomplish than we can imagine. However, after examining our present position, we would be able to identify the results of our thinking and realize the destruction of our thoughts. We will also learn how to guard them from ever slipping back again. Comfort of the body has always been our first priority. In this book, nonetheless, the ease of the mind is the focus that ultimately gives you comfort of the body. Comfort of the mind also brings with it the following rewards:

- A substantial enhancement and control of well-being and physical appearance
- A growing aptitude for cheerfulness
- An incapability to worry or fear
- A gaining of recognition
- Freedom from monotony

THE BOOK OF HEBREWS

Prayer from the Bible

Thou hast loved righteousness, and hated iniquity; therefore God, even thy God, hath anointed thee with the oil of gladness more than Your companions. And, Thou, Lord, in the beginning hast laid the foundation of the earth; and the heavens are the works of thine hands: They shall perish; but thou remainest; and they all shall wax old as doth a garment. (Hebrews 1:9-11)

Companion comes from a word that means "close associates" or "partners." The concept of the believers being companions with Christ is key in this book of Hebrews.

An Aid to Your New Path

This book is for seekers of truth. It is an aid to those new to this path. Truth can only be understood when we are in a state of mind of attention. As a result, truth is not available to us if our minds are not conditioned to receive it. Figuratively speaking, truth can only be found at the bottom of a well. And we know a well is a very deep and dark place. This is telling us that truth must be sought after and come upon with earnest effort. Also, we must dig deep in pursuit of truth. This book will prepare our mind for that truth that we seek.

In our quest for truth, we will look from within and in the Bible. Whereas this book is not an interpretation of the Bible, the Bible is used as a resource throughout the book. Why the Bible? The Bible is the book of life. It tells humans how to function while on this planet called Earth. It also depicts the promises of God. It details God's systems. And it is those principles and systems in spiritual law that will be referenced. One cannot understand God; however, one can understand His systems. In essence, this book is in part an attempt to cleanse from within. It is an effort to help us keep our minds from rubbish and poisonous material.

Power Can Be Acquired

We are told that the achievement of wisdom and power can only be acquired through study and knowledge of ourselves. We also know that there are laws governing this universe. Furthermore, we know that the same laws that govern man govern the whole universe. Where does one find those laws?

Those laws are embedded in the scripture. However, one must receive the revelation of the scriptures in order to experience their true interpretations.

The Bible is a mystery to those who don't understand it, and as a consequence, many definitions and interpretations will be given to the sections of scripture cited. Also, included throughout this book are prayers taken from the Bible. The purpose is to keep the reader focused on the promises of God as it all speaks to who you are in this body. The quotes and study scriptures in this book are referenced from the King James Version.

THE BOOK OF HEBREWS

Prayer from the Bible

And as a vesture shalt thou fold them up, and they shall be changed: but thou art the same, and thy years shall not fail. But to which of the angels said he at any time, Sit on my right hand, until I make thine enemies thy footstool? Are they not all ministering spirits, sent forth to minister for them who shall be heirs of salvation? (Hebrews 1:12-14)

It is the view of the writer that verse 14 depicts one of God's purposes for man on this earth (Are they not all ministering spirits . . . ?), "ministering" in the sense of doing good for your fellow man.

Profound Depths

In conjunction to the scriptures cited throughout the text, the Epistle to the Hebrews embodies every other page. Why the book of Hebrews? Throughout the epistle, the author stresses the connection and flow between the Old Testament revelation and the new faith in Christ. This is demonstrated while emphasizing the superiority of both Christ and His covenant. Also the style of the epistle is one of encouragement, ease, and caution. The book of Hebrews leads us from shallow thinking to profound depths concerning the work of Christ.

THE BOOK OF HEBREWS

Prayer from the Bible

Therefore we ought to give the more earnest heed to the things which we have heard, lest at any time we should let them slip. For if the word spoken by angels was stedfast, and every transgression and disobedience received a just recompence of reward; How shall we escape, if we neglect so great salvation; which at the first began to be spoken by the Lord, and was confirmed unto us by them that heard him; God also bearing them witness, both with signs and wonders, and with divers miracles, and gifts of the Holy Ghost, according to his own will? (Hebrews 2:1-4)

The book of Hebrews contains five warning passages, the first in verses 1-4. This passage warns us not to neglect Christ's message. Since God has no greater messenger than His Son, we must learn to listen to the voice within.

CHAPTER 1

In the Beginning

Many theologians and writers of spiritual works start with the Bible as this book on life details the beginning of time. To address the question, who are you? we also go to the first book in the Bible, the book of Genesis. We start here because a chief feature of Genesis is the eminently acceptable way in which it answers one's questions on origins. The book of Genesis is accurately described as the book of beginnings. It may be divided into two main parts. The first part is concerned with the early history of mankind. While the second part deals with history of the specific people whom God chose as His own. Our interest as it pertains to the question, who are you? is chapter 1 verse 1, which states,

> In the beginning God created the heaven and the earth.
> And the earth was without form, and void. (Genesis 1:1-2)

Creation of the Absolute

"In the beginning God created" marks the creation of the absolute beginning of the temporal and material world. This segment of the Bible is important in the understanding of who we are. It is also vital that we concentrate on each word as it gives intelligibility to one's identification. As one meditates on these verses, several things are noted. First, we see in the beginning "God created." That word "created" is significant. It denotes action; it also denotes creation. The second considerable note one ought to

THE BOOK OF HEBREWS

Prayer from the Bible

For unto the angels hath he not put in subjection the world to come, whereof we speak. But one in a certain place testified, saying, What is man, that thou art mindful of him? or the son of man that thou visitest him? Thou madest him a little lower than the angels; thou crownedst him with glory and honour, and didst set him over the works of thy hands: sufferings. For both he that sanctifieth and they who are sanctified are all of one: for which cause he is not ashamed to call them brethren. (Hebrews 2:5-7, 11)

Here we see the scripture outlining that man's present status does not suggest that he will someday be over all creation. However, Christ's status does. We can therefore submit to the Christ within.

observe is the earth was without "form and void." Unformed" and "unfilled" describes the condition of the earth after the initial act of creation. It does not describe a muddled condition as a result of judgment. The word "form" also plays an important part in self identification and purpose. Without form means just that, without form, in essence there was vastness, nothingness and nonexistence As we continue to examine excerpts from the Book of Genesis, we come to verse 25:

> And God made the beast of the earth after his kind and cattle after their kind, and every thing that creepeth upon the earth after his kind: and God saw that it was good. (Genesis 1:25)

Understanding of Self

The words of importance here that would aid in our understanding of self are "after his kind." Here we see God made the beasts of the earth after "their kind." As we meditate on this verse, it tells us that dogs begot dogs, cows begot cows, and goats begot goats. This again is momentous and fundamental to our perception of who we are and who we belong to. Since we now know that we are not beasts of the earth, it is imperative that we do not allow any comparison of our person to that of a beast. Now that we have covered the creation of the beasts, let us move on to chapter 1 verse 26 in the book of Genesis:

> And God said, let us make man in our image, after our likeness.

Here, we see man was created in both the image and likeness of God. The terms "image" and "likeness" are used synonymously and refer primarily to man's spiritual resemblance to his maker. In order to fully comprehend the interpretation of this verse, we must have an understanding of who and what is God? No one can fully understand God.

THE BOOK OF HEBREWS

Prayer from the Bible

Thou hast put all things in subjection under his feet. For in that he put all in subjection under him, he left nothing that is not put under him. But now we see not yet all things put under him. But we see Jesus, who was made a little lower than the angels for the suffering of death, crowned with glory and honour; that he by the grace of God should taste death for every man. (Hebrews 2:8-9)

These verses in the scripture seem to outline three reasons for Christ's sufferings: to identify with humanity, to destroy the power of death, and to become an intercessory high priest.

God Is Omnipotent

It is unattainable for our human minds to conjure up the vastness of God. God is infinite. God is love. God is omnipotent. God is the beginning and the end. God is all in all. God is. However, we could have an understanding of God's laws and systems. This is compulsory since we are made in his image and after his likeness. Then it stands to reason if we have some understanding of the Father, we would have some understanding of the sons and daughters of God. To put it purely, God is spirit. If God is spirit, then we are spirit. That is what Genesis chapter 1 is telling us.

And God said; let us make man in our image, after our likeness.

You are Spirit

An image is a representation or replica of one person or thing by another. The term "likeness" is used as gauge of comparison, or analogy. So here, we have a partial answer to our first question of who we are. Well, according to the book of Genesis, you are spirit. It is imperative that one fully understands that we are spirit. My mentor, Bishop Jordan, puts it this way: "You are a walking, talking spirit." You may want to pause and meditate on what it means to be a walking, talking spirit. It is a necessary element when addressing the question of who we are.

What? Know ye not that your body is the temple of the Holy Ghost which is in you, which ye have of God and ye are not your own? (1 Corinthians 6:19)

THE BOOK OF HEBREWS

Prayer from the Bible

For it became him, for whom are all things, and by whom are all things, in bringing many sons unto glory, to make the captain of their salvation perfect through sufferings. For both He who sanctifies and those who are being sanctified are all of one, for which reason He is not ashamed to call them brethren, Saying, I will declare thy name unto my brethren, in the midst of the church will I sing praise unto thee. And again, I will put my trust in him. And again, Behold I and the children which God hath given me. (Hebrews 2:10-13)

The Greek word for "captain" means "leader" or "originator." The word describes a pioneer. Jesus's sinless life has blazed a path to God. The phrase "all for one" refers to the fact that Jesus and all believers belong to God because the children of God and the Son himself are all from the same Father, the same Creator.

While this is a wonderful discovery, there is another body to consider—the human body.

Our Bodies Are Temples of the Holy Ghost

"Your body is the temple of the Holy Ghost." Not only is the local church a temple of the Holy Spirit, but the individual believer's body itself also is a temple of the Holy Spirit. You are spirit; however, in order to function on planet Earth one is encapsulated in human flesh. What is this human body? Why was it manifested? What do the scriptures say about the human body? In 1 Corinthians, the Bible tells us that our bodies are temples of the Holy Ghost. This is an awesome revelation. My body is the temple of the Holy Ghost. We should pause and reflect on that statement for a moment. Let the revelation of what it means to you consume your very being. In essence, just relax and soak it all in. Take some deep breaths and contemplate what this means to you. We see further acknowledgement of this in 2 Corinthians 6:16.

> And what agreement hath the temple of God with idols? For ye are the temple of the living God; as God hath said, I will dwell in them, and walk in them; and I will be their God, and they shall be my people. (2 Corinthians 6:16)

In 2 Corinthians 6:16, it goes much deeper. Here it states, "as God hath said, I will dwell in them, and walk in them." This once again supports the concept of the walking and talking spirit. God said he will walk and dwell in them. So here it is clearly established in the words of God that the human body is the temple of the Holy Ghost. This all speaks to the question of who we are. Now, let's recapitulate a little. So far, you found out that you are a spirit residing in a human body. This is great progress. However, before understanding fully who you are, you need to understand your other bodies.

THE BOOK OF HEBREWS

Prayer from the Bible

For as much then as the children are partakers of flesh and blood, he also himself likewise took part of the same; that through death he might destroy him that had the power of death, that is, the devil; And deliver them who through fear of death were all their lifetime subject to bondage. For verily he took not on him the nature of angels; but he took on him the seed of Abraham. (Hebrews 2:14-16)

Here we see these verses saying two things. Having established the unity between the Son and believers, the chapter concludes that there are two purposes of this close identification: the Son became human so that He could destroy the devil and release those who were in bondage to sin.

Whatever our devils are, we have the power within to destroy it and release ourselves from bondage.

Precipitation in Physical Matter

The physical body you see every morning in the mirror is only the densest of your seven bodies. It is the precipitation in physical matter of all your aspirations, achievements, and weaknesses of many embodiments. It is the effect of thousands of causes you created in your past lives and in this one. Throughout this journey all seven bodies will be discovered. Please note that only a simplistic description of the seven bodies of man will be portrayed. It is not the intent of the writer to provide study literature on this subject matter, just to identify it and give a brief overview. Now let us look at the human body.

The human organism, as we know it, is composed of seven distinct bodies, all invisible except the physical. These bodies are divided into two groupings, which we will refer to as the "higher self" and the "lower self." The higher three bodies represent the spiritually in man while the lower four, being of the world of form, are connected while man lives in physical form. The connection of these two groupings—higher and lower—creates the human organism as we know it and makes man able to come in contact with the lower kingdom of nature as well as those higher spiritual values.

THE BOOK OF HEBREWS

Prayer from the Bible

Wherefore in all things it behoved him to be made like unto his brethren, that he might be a merciful and faithful high priest in things pertaining to God, to make reconciliation for the sins of the people. For in that he himself hath suffered being tempted, he is able to succour them that are tempted. (Hebrews 2:17-18)

The word "succour" means "to come to the aid of" someone.

The Human Brain

The Eastern explanations of the seven bodies of awareness result from a subjective feeling and not an objective test. It is therefore advised that you take these descriptions as individual states of awareness, not as proven physical science. The human brain contains approximately 100 billion neurons, all connected by an estimated 50 trillion synapses. This deep sea of electrified living cells creates the natural holographic phenomenon we know as consciousness. The amount of variation in human consciousness is almost infinite because all those neurons and synapses can fire in an essentially infinite number of sequences. No two humans have exactly the same brain structure, and no two moments in any individual's consciousness are ever exactly the same.

THE BOOK OF HEBREWS

Prayer from the Bible

Wherefore, holy brethren, partakers of the heavenly calling, consider the Apostle and High Priest of our profession, Christ Jesus; Who was faithful to him that appointed him, as also Moses was faithful in all his house. For this man was counted worthy of more glory than Moses, inasmuch as he who hath builded the house hath more honour than the house. (Hebrews 3:1-3)

The scripture is clearly telling us that Christ is man's direct intercessor.

CHAPTER 2

The Seven Bodies of Man

Humankind (man) according to many is a sevenfold being, or one can say man's nature has seven aspects/bodies. Whatever words may be used, the information remains the same that man is essentially sevenfold and an evolving being. However, the clearest way to think of man is to regard him as one spirit. This is a very deep subject and needs detailed attention. In this chapter, however, it is not the intent of the writer to show relationships between the seven bodies of man. Nonetheless, our discussion is on identifying the seven aspects/bodies of man, as we have already determined that man is spirit, and consciousness is all there is. A glossary of terms is provided at the end of the book to define some of the unusual terms. The first of the seven bodies is the physical body.

The Physical Body

The most obvious and first of the seven bodies of man is his dense physical body. This material part or nature of a human being is composed of five senses. Its organs of locomotion, the brain and nervous system are the machinery necessary for carrying on the various functions for continued existence. This body possesses the same material as in the physical world. This solid physical body of low-frequency vibrations is like an apparatus or switchboard through which man contacts physical things. This physical body interpenetrated by another body called the etheric body is the second of man's seven bodies.

THE BOOK OF HEBREWS

Prayer from the Bible

Wherefore I was grieved with that generation, and said, They do always err in their heart; and they have not known my ways. So I sware in my wrath, They shall not enter into my rest.) Take heed, brethren, lest there be in any of you an evil heart of unbelief, in departing from the living God. But exhort one another daily, while it is called To day; lest any of you be hardened through the deceitfulness of sin. (Hebrews 3:10-13)

The Etheric Body

The etheric body, the ethereal body, the fluidic body, the double, and the wraith, are all names by which this second body of man is called. This etheric body, which is made up of four ethers, is still physical but not visible for the majority of humankind. It is said to be like a violet gray mist or fine web covering our physical body. This mist or fine web is believed to be the electric and radiating life forces through which the physical body is fed from the outer universe. In essence, this body operating at higher and finer vibrations acts as a channel through which all the magnetic life forces are fed. The etheric body completes our physical plane equipment. The etheric may be more recognizable by the term "man's double." The third of the seven bodies is the astral body.

Astral Body

The astral body is matter, yet it is composed of material that is unfamiliar to us. It cannot be perceived by the gross physical senses and has none of the attributes used to define substances in physics. However, it can be perceived by finer senses and therefore can be considered matter. One can say it is an older and more evolved kind of matter.

The astral body protrudes outside the physical body and is used by clairvoyants to describe a person. The astral body's matter is said to possess a very fine texture as compared with the visible body and has great tensile strength. And not only does it have this mammoth strength, but it at the same time possesses an elasticity permitting it to extend considerable distance. It is flexible, plastic, extensible, and strong. The matter of which it is composed is electrical and magnetic in its essence. Our astral body interpenetrates the other two bodies, and it can travel when polarized entirely, for example when we sleep. The astral body cannot, in the case of ordinary people, travel more than a few feet from the physical body, which it does during sleep or reverie.

THE BOOK OF HEBREWS

Prayer from the Bible

For we are made partakers of Christ, if we hold the beginning of our confidence stedfast unto the end; While it is said, To day if ye will hear his voice, harden not your hearts, as in the provocation. For some, when they had heard, did provoke: howbeit not all that came out of Egypt by Moses. (Hebrews 3:14-16)

The Mental Body

The mental body receives ideas and impressions from the mental plane. These ideas can also come as promptings from the Holy Christ Self. The brains receive thoughts from the mental body; they do not create thoughts themselves. Just as the computer doesn't create by itself, so is the brain programmed by the mental body. It is a tool in the hands of your consciousness. In an effort to explain the next three bodies, the author will use the Catholic explanation of the Trinity to try and illuminate the concept that the Father, the Son, and the Holy Spirit as one and the same God. It should be noted, however, that the Trinity this divine economy is a mystery. As a result, it cannot be explained but must be experienced.

The Trinity

The Trinity refers to God threefold in being. This divine Trinity is known as Father, Son, and Holy Spirit. Metaphysically, these refer to mind, idea, and expression. The Catholics express it this way. To believe in the Holy Spirit is to profess that the Holy Spirit is one of the persons of the Holy Trinity, consubstantial with the Father and the Son; with the Father and the Son He is worshipped and glorified. For this reason, the divine mystery of the Holy Spirit was already treated in the context of Trinitarian theology. Here, however, we are concerned with the Holy Spirit only in the divine economy.

From the beginning through to the completion of the plan for our salvation, the Holy Spirit is at work with the Father and the Son. But in these "end times" ushered in by the Son's redeeming incarnation, the Spirit is revealed and given, recognized and welcomed as a person. In essence, the Holy Spirit was at work all along, but only discovered following the Son's personification.

> The mystery which has been hidden from the ages and from generations but now has been revealed to His saints. Christ in you, the hope of Glory. (Colossians 1:26-27)

THE BOOK OF HEBREWS

Prayer from the Bible

For every house is builded by some man; but he that built all things is God. And Moses verily was faithful in all his house, as a servant, for a testimony of those things which were to be spoken after; But Christ as a son over his own house; whose house are we, if we hold fast the confidence and the rejoicing of the hope firm unto the end. Wherefore (as the Holy Ghost saith, To day if ye will hear his voice, Harden not your hearts, as in the provocation, in the day of temptation in the wilderness: When your fathers tempted me, proved me, and saw my works forty years. (Hebrews 3:4-9)

The Catholic teachings further state that no one comprehends the thoughts of God, except the Spirit of God. Now God's Spirit, who reveals God, makes known to us Christ, the Word, his living utterance, but the Spirit does not speak of himself. The Spirit who has spoken through the prophets makes us hear the Father's word, but we do not hear the Spirit himself. We know him only in the movement by which he reveals the Word to us and disposes us to welcome him in faith. The Spirit of Truth who unveils Christ to us will not speak on his own. Such properly divine self-effacement explains why "the world cannot receive him, because it neither sees him nor knows him" while those who believe in Christ know the Spirit because he dwells within them.

The One whom the Father has sent into our hearts, the Spirit of his Son, is truly God. Consubstantial with the Father and the Son, the Spirit is inseparable from them, in both the inner life of the Trinity and his gift of love for the world. In adoring the Holy Trinity—life-giving, consubstantial, and indivisible—the church's faith also professes the distinction of person. When the Father sends his word, he always sends his breath. In their joint mission, the Son and the Holy Spirit are distinct but inseparable.

Before wrapping up this section on the seven bodies of man and the Holy Trinity, let's look at Trinitarian spirituality in an effort to understand the power within us.

But it pleased God, to reveal His son in me. (Galatians 1:15-16)

THE BOOK OF HEBREWS

Prayer from the Bible

But with whom was he grieved forty years? Was it not with them that had sinned, whose carcases fell in the wilderness? And to whom sware he that they should not enter into his rest, but to them that believed not? So we see that they could not enter in because of unbelief. (Hebrews 3:17-19)

Trinitarian Spirituality

The Christian East has always understood spirituality as an intimate relationship of the individual or the church with God the Father through the incarnate Son of God, Jesus Christ, and in the Holy Spirit. It has always been a liturgical spirituality based on the glorification of the most Holy Trinity through the divine Liturgy and of the holy sacraments.

The triadic (one in which the number of places in the relation is three) content of this spirituality is based on the teaching that the Trinity is the ultimate beginning of all creatures through the act of creation out of nothing. The entire cosmos is an image of the most Holy Trinity. Therefore, it is triadophoric reality, bearing the likeness and seal of the Trinity. Since the visible and invisible cosmos in its entirety exists in the ubiquitous triadic God who is the ground of its being, it is totally dependent on Him for both its existence and its operation.

For this reason, the total cosmic reality is triadocentric. Furthermore, the whole cosmos, in its tremendous energy, is a triadophorical reality for it tends toward the most Holy Trinity as its perfect goal, the omega point. So what does it all mean? In its most general sense, a cosmos is an orderly or harmonious system. In essence, this harmonious system (cosmos) tendency is toward the Most Holy Trinity as its perfect goal. As we conclude chapter 2, let us meditate on a few verses taken from the book of Romans.

THE BOOK OF HEBREWS

Prayer from the Bible

Let us therefore fear, lest, a promise being left us of entering into his rest, any of you should seem to come short of it. 2 For unto us was the gospel preached, as well as unto them: but the word preached did not profit them, not being mixed with faith in them that heard it. 3 For we which have believed do enter into rest, as he said, As I have sworn in my wrath, if they shall enter into my rest: although the works were finished from the foundation of the world. (Hebrews 4:1-3)

Meditation

So then, they that are in the flesh cannot please God. But ye are not in the flesh, but in the Spirit, if so be that the Spirit of God dwell in you. Now if any man have not the Spirit of Christ, he is none of his. And if Christ be in you, the body is dead because of sin; but the Spirit is life because of righteousness. But if the Spirit of him that raised up Jesus from the dead dwell in you, he that raised up Christ from the dead shall also quicken your mortal bodies by his Spirit that dwelleth in you. Therefore, brethren, we are debtors, not to the flesh, to live after the flesh. For if ye live after the flesh, ye shall die: but if ye through the Spirit do mortify the deeds of the body, ye shall live. For as many as are led by the Spirit of God, they are the sons of God. For ye have not received the spirit of bondage again to fear; but ye have received the Spirit of adoption, whereby we cry, Abba, Father. The Spirit itself beareth witness with our spirit, that we are the children of God: And if children, then heirs; heirs of God, and joint-heirs with Christ; if so be that we suffer with him, that we may be also glorified together. (Romans 8:8-17)

THE BOOK OF HEBREWS

Prayers from the Bible

For he spake in a certain place of the seventh day on this wise, And God did rest the seventh day from all his works. And in this place again, If they shall enter into my rest. Seeing therefore it remaineth that some must enter therein, and they to whom it was first preached entered not in because of unbelief: Again, he limiteth a certain day, saying in David, To day, after so long a time; as it is said, To day if ye will hear his voice, harden not your hearts. For if Jesus had given them rest, then would he not afterward have spoken of another day. There remaineth therefore a rest to the people of God. For he that is entered into his rest, he also hath ceased from his own works, as God did from his. Let us labour therefore to enter into that rest, lest any man fall after the same example of unbelief. (Hebrews 4:4-11)

CHAPTER 3

You Are the Sum Total of Your Thoughts

The scientists say that human thought travel one hundred eighty-six thousand miles per second, nine hundred thirty thousand times faster than the sound of our voice. It is quite evident then that we do not articulate most of our thoughts, yet they determine what we are and what we are becoming. We may not voice a particular thought, but the mere fact that we think it means it will affect our lives. We may think that we can let our minds wander off to all sorts of negative places and things without any negative impact on our bodies. After all, it is just our thoughts. They are not hurting anyone. Well, nothing could be further from reality because negative thinking is very damaging. It is damaging to our bodies our minds and our manifestations (in the mystical traditions, the *manifest*, or being, is that which exists). In this section, we are going to address our thoughts as they speak to our identity. The Old Testament in the book of Genesis 6:5 states,

> And God saw that the wickedness of man was great in the earth, and that every imagination of the thought of his heart was only evil continually.

THE BOOK OF HEBREWS

Prayer from the Bible

For the word of God is quick, and powerful, and sharper than any two-edged sword, piercing even to the dividing asunder of soul and spirit, and of the joints and marrow, and is a discerner of the thoughts and intents of the heart. 13 Neither is there any creature that is not manifest in his sight: but all things are naked and opened unto the eyes of him with whom we have to do. (Hebrews 4:12-13)

Everything Begins with Thought

Then we see in the New Testament where the Bible explains it further and unmistakably tells us what defiles a man. Matthew in the New Testament is telling us we must learn to control our thoughts. Everything begins with a thought. The conditions you are facing right now materialized from your thoughts. Every so-called problem we encounter first originated from our thoughts. This book of life tells you what one's thoughts are capable of producing. Matthew 15:19 explains what thoughts can produce:

> For out of the heart proceed evil thoughts, murders, adulteries, fornications, thefts, false witness, and blasphemies: Matthew Chapter15 Verse 19

Evil schemes flow from evil thoughts. Also, blasphemies refer not only to blasphemy in the narrow modern sense of the word, but also to criticism or libel of others. It does not end there. Proverbs 18:21 puts it this way:

> Death and life are in the power of the tongue.

You Are the Compilation of Your Thoughts

You are the compilation of all your thoughts. In essence, you are what you think. You are what you pay mind to. One doesn't have to be clairvoyant to know what is on a person's mind. One only has to look at their surroundings to get a window into their mind. Whatever you pay mind to will manifest in your life. Observing a person's habits and observing who their friends are can paint a clear picture of their identity. My mentor puts it this way: "your friends are your prophecy." They tell you where you are heading. The book of life also outlines clearly what the content of one thought should be. Philippians 4:8 puts it this way:

> Finally, brethren, whatsoever things are true, whatsoever things are just, whatsoever things are pure, whatsoever things are lovely, whatsoever things are of good report; if there be any virtue, and if there be any praise, think on these things.

THE BOOK OF HEBREWS

Prayer from the Bible

Seeing then that we have a great high priest, that is passed into the heavens, Jesus the Son of God, let us hold fast our profession. For we have not an high priest which cannot be touched with the feeling of our infirmities; but was in all points tempted like as we are, yet without sin. Let us therefore come boldly unto the throne of grace, that we may obtain mercy, and find grace to help in time of need. (Hebrews 4:14-16)

Every Action Has a Preceding Thought

The scriptures are saying in order to keep God's peace; people must occupy their minds with the right things and busy themselves with the right activities. Here we see the Bible saying that there is power in words, there is power in thought, and thoughts determine what is manifested in this earthly realm. The Bible offers these words of caution because all action is the result of thought. Whatever you are doing right now first appeared as a thought in your mind whether you were aware of the thought or not. Every action has a preceding thought. Nothing is acted upon unless it first appeared as a thought in the mind. We can no longer afford the luxury of unorganized thoughts. We must practice correct thinking.

When we practice correct thinking, we attract the right action and obtain the right results. These truths not only alert us to pay attention to our thoughts, but also place a tremendous burden on us to accept responsibility for our present circumstances. This is a tall order as it is very easy to blame something or someone outside of you for your present predicament. However, do not panic; the same way you thought yourself into this dilemma, you can think yourself out of it.

THE BOOK OF HEBREWS

Prayer from the Bible

For every high priest taken from among men is ordained for men in things pertaining to God, that he may offer both gifts and sacrifices for sins: Who can have compassion on the ignorant, and on them that are out of the way; for that he himself also is compassed with infirmity. And by reason hereof he ought, as for the people, so also for himself, to offer for sins. (Hebrews 5:1-3)

Thoughts Are Seeds We Plant

Who are you? You are your thoughts, and your thoughts are you. You are what you think all day long. In essence, you are the sum total of your thoughts. It is extremely important to be in command of one's thoughts and to not allow the mind to drift down an unconstructive street. We must remember that like attracts like. As a result, whatever thoughts are in our mind that is what we manifest.

An occurrence from my youth comes to mind. A soccer club from a major city was visiting our city for the first time. At night a group of us took the players out for dinner to one of my favorite restaurants. The area of town where the restaurant was located is one that I frequented. I felt safe there and never observed any illicit activities. However, in a matter of minutes after arriving at the eatery, a member of the visiting soccer team was able to purchase prohibited pharmaceutical on the street. This made an impression on me as I never observed such activities in that part of town. This illustrates the idea that you will find what you seek. It is also an illustration of how like attracts like. Galatians chapter 6 verse 7 puts it this way:

Whatsoever a man soweth, that he also reap. (Galatians Chapter 6)

The seeking first occurs in the mind. In essence, thoughts are seeds we plant in our minds.

THE BOOK OF HEBREWS

Prayer from the Bible

And no man taketh this honour unto himself, but he that is called of God, as was Aaron. So also Christ glorified not himself to be made an high priest; but he that said unto him, Thou art my Son, to day have I begotten thee. As he saith also in another place, Thou art a priest for ever after the order of Melchisedec. (Hebrews 5:4-6)

Communicating Your Thoughts

"Soweth" means "does" or "practices." Reap could also be said as "be requited" or "recompensed." Your thoughts about yourself will expand out into the world. In essence, we communicate with our thoughts. We communicate with our thoughts by just thinking them. If your thoughts do not match your spoken words, you may deceive someone for a time; however, they will always have an uneasy feeling about you. In essence, we can deceive someone with our words but not with our thoughts. This nonverbal communication is very powerful. Consequently, it is wise to be aware that you are communicating those prevailing thoughts that are playing around in your head. Your thoughts are an expression of you. As a matter of speaking, your thoughts are you. The book of Proverbs puts it in this fashion:

For as he thinketh in his heart, so is he. (Proverbs 23:7)

For As He Thinketh So Is He

"For as he thinketh in his heart, so is he." This is also saying whatever you sow in your mind and heart will bear fruit. In essence, it will manifest as oneself. What thoughts you deposit in your mind will grow. It is your thoughts; it is your thoughts shaping you into the person you are becoming. We are always evolving, and our thoughts are the catalyst for this process. Your thoughts form you, and you form your thoughts. So it makes sense that if you are the sum total of your thoughts, then you have the ability to become whatever you want.

THE BOOK OF HEBREWS

Prayer from the Bible

Who in the days of his flesh, when he had offered up prayers and supplications with strong crying and tears unto him that was able to save him from death, and was heard in that he feared; Though he were a Son, yet learned he obedience by the things which he suffered; And being made perfect, he became the author of eternal salvation unto all them that obey him; Called of God an high priest after the order of Melchisedec. (Hebrews 5:7-10)

Putting that aside for a moment, it is well established scientifically that the body of man is moved by his mind. It is through our thoughts process that we control the movement of our body. Your thoughts also affect how you see. As we conclude chapter 3, let us reflect on a few verses from 1 Corinthians:

> For as the body is one, and hath many members, and all the members of that one body, being many, are one body: so also is Christ. For by one Spirit are we all baptized into one body, whether we be Jews or Gentiles, whether we be bond or free; and have been all made to drink into one Spirit. For the body is not one member, but many. (1 Corinthians 12:12-4)

THE BOOK OF HEBREWS

Prayer from the Bible

Of whom we have many things to say, and hard to be uttered, seeing ye are dull of hearing. For when for the time ye ought to be teachers, ye have need that one teach you again which be the first principles of the oracles of God; and are become such as have need of milk, and not of strong meat. For every one that useth milk is unskilful in the word of righteousness: for he is a babe. But strong meat belongeth to them that are of full age, even those who by reason of use have their senses exercised to discern both good and evil. (Hebrews 5:11-14)

CHAPTER 4

What Are You Seeing?

What are you seeing? What we see reflects what we are thinking, and we are what we think. Since we are what we think and what we see affects our thinking, how do one control what one sees? First, it is essential to comprehend that everyone sees through their mind and not their eyes. In essence, we see through our mind's eye. Therefore, thoughts affect the way we see. Also, what we believe determines what we see. This statement is true for all of us. Two people can look at the same object and see two very different things.

Our Mental Picture

It is imperative to grasp this concept as it also relates to how we name things. We often name or call things according to the circumstances that exist at the time. Being conscious of how our thoughts are affected will help to clarify of our mental picture. Having clear vision allows one the opportunity to call things accurately. We name a thing based on our considerations about it at that particular time. Also, how we name a thing reflects how we interact with that entity. The book of Genesis chapter 2 tells us that God brought all living creatures to be named by Adam.

> brought them unto Adam to see what he would call them; and whatsoever Adam called every living creature, that was the name thereof. (Genesis 2:19)

THE BOOK OF HEBREWS

Prayer from the Bible

Therefore leaving the principles of the doctrine of Christ, let us go on unto perfection; not laying again the foundation of repentance from dead works, and of faith toward God, Of the doctrine of baptisms, and of laying on of hands, and of resurrection of the dead, and of eternal judgment. (Hebrews 6:1-2)

This is God delegating authority to man since the act of naming the animals shows lordship or dominion. The scripture is telling us we have the ability, the power, and the dominion to name our situations. It is vital that we feel love before we name a thing, a situation, a circumstances, and so on. God did not change the names Adam gave to every living creature. Whatever we call it, that is what it becomes to us.

Emotional Attachment

God will not change the way we choose to see. We have a tendency to name things based on our past experience and emotional attachment. Very often we allow our emotions to control our thoughts, our thinking, and ultimately our sight. How often do we formulate a view based on someone else's impression? How often have we allowed ourselves to absorb the emotions of others, thereby letting their energy infiltrate our mind, thoughts, and consciousness?

This all speaks to the importance of seeing with one's inner eye. Sight lies in one's consciousness. One's sight is based on one's knowledge of the thing. From birth we were bombarded with images of objects. In this world of mass communication we are further saturated with images of scarcity and devastation. All of this helps to form our thoughts and, consequently, what we think and see. Our thoughts then form who we are. Sometimes it may be necessary to correct old impressions. We may have to rename some of our experiences in order to move forward and avoid repeating the same experiences.

Old experiences often come back to alter your present. If we do not rename them, we tend to live in the past. And if that past was negative, it will impact negatively on our present and who we are.

THE BOOK OF HEBREWS

Prayer from the Bible

And this will we do, if God permit. For it is impossible for those who were once enlightened, and have tasted of the heavenly gift, and were made partakers of the Holy Ghost. (Hebrews 6 3-4)

The Mental Image

Mental images are formed when something significant happens in our life. As new similar experiences occur, we tend to react according to the mental image stored in our minds. Correcting old impressions is not an easy fix. It takes time, for one must be continually renewing one's mind and thoughts. First awareness of the past hurt must be recognized in order to be renamed. If these thoughts, impressions, and mental images of yesteryear are not corrected, they can stunt one's growth. In essence, we will be trapped in the past like a car tire stuck in the mud rolling and getting nowhere. Romans 12:2 puts it this way:

> And be not conformed to this world: but be ye transformed by the renewing of your mind, that ye may prove what is good, and acceptable, and perfect, will of God. (Romans 12:2)

"Be not conformed" means to stop conforming. You are to resist the present day thinking, value systems, and conduct of this world. We each want the very best life has to offer. As a result, we work hard with all our capacity in order to succeed. However, our best efforts can be wasted if we allow negative thoughts from the past to intrude into our present.

The problem of a lack of success, however, lies in ones thought process. The past will emerge to influence our present if it is not reversed. Past images if not cleaned up and renamed, could be blocking growth. It could also block or alter the image of your true self.

THE BOOK OF HEBREWS

Prayer from the Bible

And have tasted the good word of God, and the powers of the world to come, If they shall fall away, to renew them again unto repentance; seeing they crucify to themselves the Son of God afresh, and put him to an open shame. For the earth which drinketh in the rain that cometh oft upon it, and bringeth forth herbs meet for them by whom it is dressed, receiveth blessing from God: But that which beareth thorns and briers is rejected, and is nigh unto cursing; whose end is to be burned. (Hebrews 6:5-8)

I Deemed Myself As Having a Weight Problem

It is difficult not to be affected by ones surroundings even with the knowledge that we see with our mine's eye. For example, in the world's view and in my own mind, I thought I had a weight problem. Even when I weighed ninety-nine pounds, I still felt overweight. I had to go within and conduct a self-examination to determine where I picked up that concept. It was revealed to me that for many years as a child I was told that I would be fat like my aunt. This thought became embedded in my consciousnesses and tormented me for a very long time. However, recognizing the source of the torment means I can now forgive and can thereby alter my past and present.

Being bombarded with negative images and poverty every day would have an impact on anyone's thoughts. It's like throwing mud on a wall. While most of it might fall off, some would stick. How do we prevent our perception of present negative circumstances from altering and eventually damaging our thoughts? This is done by the renewing of one's mind as often as necessary.

> For which cause we faint not; but though our outward man perish, yet the inward man is renewed day by day. (2 Corinthians 4:16)

Ten times a day if that is what it takes. You are what you think. What are you thinking?

THE BOOK OF HEBREWS

Prayer from the Bible

But, beloved, we are persuaded better things of you, and things that accompany salvation, though we thus speak. For God is not unrighteous to forget your work and labour of love, which ye have shewed toward his name, in that ye have ministered to the saints, and do minister. And we desire that every one of you do shew the same diligence to the full assurance of hope unto the end: That ye be not slothful, but followers of them who through faith and patience inherit the promises. (Hebrews 6:9-12)

CHAPTER 5

What Records Are You Playing?

Who are you? Are you a product of your past experiences? How strong are the influences of your parents on your current thoughts? Do incidents and circumstances of the past contribute to your present philosophy and ideology? Are the words of your parents, your grandparents, your teachers, and all who spoke into your ear from the beginning of conception affecting the decisions you make today? These are all factors that can impact your life. If these records or tapes are negative, you could find yourself in a rut. People in this situation continually make the same mistakes and attract the wrong people into their lives. Depending on the extent of the negative experience, past negative teachings can even affect your present relationships. In this chapter we are addressing those tapes that keep playing in your mind, those tapes that you would like to turn off but don't quite know how.

A Product of Our Past

We are all a product of our past. That is what helped shape us into the person we are today. Whether we want to admit it or not, the dominant people in our lives do have a significant impact on who we become as individuals. While that can be very good, it can also be an imprisonment. The good thing is one doesn't have to be incarcerated by old and negative beliefs as

THE BOOK OF HEBREWS

Prayer from the Bible

For when God made promise to Abraham, because he could swear by no greater, he sware by himself, Saying, Surely blessing I will bless thee, and multiplying I will multiply thee. And so, after he had patiently endured, he obtained the promise. For men verily swear by the greater: and an oath for confirmation is to them an end of all strife. Wherein God, willing more abundantly to shew unto the heirs of promise the immutability of his counsel, confirmed it by an oath. (Hebrews 6:13-17)

we are always being and becoming. And we can always change our current circumstances through our thought process. We all want to capture the best from our past experiences.

However, the pain and hurt often associated with that experience tend to dominate our thoughts. The key is to ensure those thoughts do not rob you of your present. To accomplish this, there are some truths about the mind that one must first understand.

The Mind Is the Battleground

The mind is the battleground. In our mind is where change must begin. Change occurs within. The mind is also our dwelling place. It is where one lives all day long. It is our habitation, and in our habitation we tend to adopt certain lifestyles, routines, traditions, rituals, and customs. Those traditions and customs all come from our thoughts. They reflect who we are and who we are becoming. Thoughts are expressed as routines, customs, and habits. In order to become the person we think we are, we must clean up our habitation. This cleaning process also addresses those lifestyle, routines, traditions, ritual, and customs that impact negatively on our present day lives. Our dwelling place must be safe, free from worry and fear. It must be a place of security for us. It must be that most high place where one could dwell. Psalm 91 puts it this way:

He that dwelleth in the secret place of the most High shall abide under the shadow of the Almighty. (Psalms 91:1)

THE BOOK OF HEBREWS

Prayer from the Bible

That by two immutable things, in which it was impossible for God to lie, we might have a strong consolation, who have fled for refuge to lay hold upon the hope set before us: Which hope we have as an anchor of the soul, both sure and stedfast, and which entereth into that within the veil. (Hebrews 6:18-19)

The key word to describe this psalm is "refuge," a place of safety. One's inward expression reflects one's outward expression. The mind can acquire a state of calm, peace, and tranquility. There are other scriptures that speak to a pleasant rest in one's mind. Psalm 23 comes to mind. It states,

> He maketh me to lie down in green pasture: he leadeth me beside the still waters. He restoreth my soul: he leadeth me in the paths of righteousness for his name's sake. Yea though I walk through the valley of the shadow of death, I will fear no evil: for thou art with me thy rod and thy staff they comfort me. (Psalm 23:2-4)

The Mind Is Its Own Place

This psalm is expressed simply as the role of God (Psalm 23) as our protector and provider in life. And our God our protector lies in us. The mind is the beginning point of everything you do. In essence, if one could gain control of one's mind, one could gain control of one's external circumstances. My mentor puts it this way: "The mind is its own place and of itself can make heaven of hell or a hell of heaven." To put it another way our mind is our own God or our own devil. It is all up to you, and how you want to name it. This is an oversimplification of course as there are spiritual laws and systems. Nonetheless, one could take hold of the idea. However, when one harbors negative or harmful thoughts one is in essence making a hell of one's present heaven.

THE BOOK OF HEBREWS

Prayer from the Bible

Whither the forerunner is for us entered, even Jesus, made an high priest for ever after the order of Melchisedec. (Hebrews 6:20)

For example, I had what the world calls dyslexia, and for many years, in spite of my learned accomplishments, I thought of myself as inadequate and not quite as intelligent as my colleagues. Through the teachings of the Master Prophet, I came to know who I am. I also know that I am blessed with superb wisdom and intelligence. Understand this: your mind has the ability to put away those thoughts that are not profitable for you.

Live in the now

Guilt, fear, and regrets can all play havoc with your thoughts and influence your emotions. Nevertheless, in order to quit the past, it is necessary to forgive. Forgiveness of oneself and of others who may have caused you pain is absolutely necessary in becoming the person you wish to be. Past pain from past experiences often lingers and influences the present, but it does not have to. Another important factor here is trying to become something out of the past; that and willing or attempting to relive the past will negatively affect our present. One can only move forward when one stops living in the past. One must get out of the past and out of the future and live in the now. We all have the ability to change and develop. This requires letting go of some of those painful and negative experiences from the past. It will also mean an end to those "pity parties" and the "poor me" syndrome.

THE BOOK OF HEBREWS

Prayer from the Bible

For this Melchisedec, king of Salem, priest of the most high God, who met Abraham returning from the slaughter of the kings, and blessed him; To whom also Abraham gave a tenth part of all; first being by interpretation King of righteousness, and after that also King of Salem, which is, King of peace; Without father, without mother, without descent, having neither beginning of days, nor end of life; but made like unto the Son of God; abideth a priest continually. Now consider how great this man was, unto whom even the patriarch Abraham gave the tenth of the spoils. (Hebrews 7:1-4)

The Mind Is a Powerful Tool

The mind is a powerful tool. If we ponder on a thing long enough, it will manifest. Suffice it to say that if there is a "pity party" going on in your mind, you will become disheartened. For example, there are people in Europe who manifested the nail marks of the crucified Jesus Christ in their bodies. Anyone can experience the same result if they spend enough time dwelling emotionally on the Passion.

This concept is applicable to everyone's thought processes. Any individual can manifest any result they desire on their bodies if they are determined to focus their thoughts and feeling on it. What you take into your mind with any measure of concentration must be converted into manifestation on the body since the mind and the body is one. We are what we imagine all day long. Individuals often make themselves sick through their thoughts. We are under the influence of our own negative thoughts and deeds, and under no other influences. We just love to blame some outside force for the circumstance in which we find ourselves, and for the person we ultimately become because of those circumstances.

The reality, however, for the majority of the time is we are the product of our own follies and responsible for the person manifested from that unwise conduct resulting from unwise thoughts. We often hear the phrase "sins of the fathers" used to explain one's negative behavior. What does it mean? We love to blame our misfortune woes, shortcomings, bad habits, and other deeds of destructions on the sins of our forefathers. While I can't address what that means in a spiritual context, I do recognize that a lot of what we experience can be fixed with right thinking. Hosea chapter 4 verse 6 puts it this way:

My people are destroyed for lack of knowledge. (Hosea 4:6)

THE BOOK OF HEBREWS

Prayer from the Bible

And verily they that are of the sons of Levi, who receive the office of the priesthood, have a commandment to take tithes of the people according to the law, that is, of their brethren, though they come out of the loins of Abraham: But he whose descent is not counted from them received tithes of Abraham, and blessed him that had the promises. And without all contradiction the less is blessed of the better. And here men that die receive tithes; but there he receiveth them, of whom it is witnessed that he liveth. And as I may so say, Levi also, who receiveth tithes, payed tithes in Abraham. (Hebrews 7:5-9)

Man's Problem Is "Lack of Knowledge"

Here the scripture is telling us the foundation of man's problem is "lack of knowledge." It does not stem from a lack of information, but rather from rejection of information. Lack of knowledge or rejection of knowledge allows us to form certain habits. We are our habits, and our habits reflect who we are. It is where we live. They are what we know and are comfortable with, be it negative or not. It is this comfort with old habits that we must change. We have all heard people complain about one thing or another; however, if you make a suggestion for a corrective action, that same person will have a million and one reasons why your suggestion would not work. The truth is they are comfortable with their situation and have no intention of changing despite their complaint.

The Old Must Die in Order to Birth the New

To be the person we think we are, we must correct our thinking. It is possible to change one's habits and as a result, one's habitation. Here is a rule of thumb I came across that works: If you would like to break a habit, do something different from the habit you are trying to break for a period of thirty days. For example, if you have a habit of taking your tea with sugar and would like to stop, take your tea without sugar for thirty days. At the end of that thirty-day period, you should no longer crave sugar in your tea. And as a result you will be well on your way to controlling that habit. We can change habits. This rule illustrates the principle that the old must die in order to birth the new. The scriptures put it this way in Matthew 9:17:

> Neither do men put new wine into old bottles: else the bottles break, and the wine runneth out, and the bottles perish: but they put new wine into new bottles, and both are preserved.

THE BOOK OF HEBREWS

Prayer from the Bible

For he was yet in the loins of his father, when Melchisedec met him. If therefore perfection were by the Levitical priesthood, (for under it the people received the law,) what further need was there that another priest should rise after the order of Melchisedec, and not be called after the order of Aaron? For the priesthood being changed, there is made of necessity a change also of the law. For he of whom these things are spoken pertaineth to another tribe, of which no man gave attendance at the altar. For it is evident that our Lord sprang out of Juda; of which tribe Moses spake nothing concerning priesthood. (Hebrews 7:10-14).

The principle expressed here is that the Lord Jesus Christ has come to bring in a whole new dispensation that cannot be fitted into forms of the old Jewish economy. This is the same standard you are trying to convey. You are bringing in a new habit that cannot fit into the old way. As a result, the old habit must die in order for the new replacement to survive. That death could occur over that thirty-day period. Knowing and then acting on this principle gives one power over the decisions one makes. By changing how you think or view a situation, you can change your negative habits, routine, practice, behavior, lifestyle for healthier ones.

THE BOOK OF HEBREWS

Prayer from the Bible

And it is yet far more evident: for that after the similitude of Melchisedec there ariseth another priest, Who is made, not after the law of a carnal commandment, but after the power of an endless life. For he testifieth, Thou art a priest for ever after the order of Melchisedec. (Hebrews 7:15-17)

CHAPTER 6

What Patterns Are You Noticing?

As we seek to discover our true self by pondering the question of who we are, we could come face to face with one's routines and habits. It may then be recognizable that these habits are dictating who we are. Based on the thirty-day principle, we now have an opportunity to shape our direction by adapting a change in our thought process. As we apply this theory, a pattern may emerge. Everything in life has a pattern. This could be a set of circumstances that leads to a particular outcome. It could also be feelings, a drawing, or a template. To help identify these, try to remember what your feelings were just before that positive outcome. What are your beliefs? What are your norms? It is significant to find the correct pattern. Throughout the scriptures we see references to the importance of patterns. In Exodus 25:9 it states,

> According to all that I show thee, after the pattern of the tabernacle, and the pattern of all the instruments thereof, even so shall ye make it.

There are fifty chapters in the Bible devoted to the tabernacle including the final sixteen chapters of Exodus. Exodus is devoted to the instructions and fashioning of the tabernacle. The amount of space dedicated certainly demonstrates its importance. This same importance must be given to one's life patterns. While we function on this earth, we do so in the course of the individual steps we perform.

THE BOOK OF HEBREWS

Prayer from the Bible

For there is verily a disannulling of the commandment going before for the weakness and unprofitableness thereof. For the law made nothing perfect, but the bringing in of a better hope did; by the which we draw nigh unto God. (Hebrews 7:18-19)

Actions Form Patterns

Consequently, those steps or actions are primary to what we are, much in the same way that particles are basic units of material. These actions form patterns, and these patterns tell a story. In essence, our actions tell a narrative about us.

To put it differently, all the energy and different aspects that exercise their authority in life and in the world are represented at the point of the individual act.

These then divulge their distinctive function at our individual level.

Another example is much the same way as an individual cell functions within an organ and then as part of a body. All this is relevant as we ponder the question of, who are you?

The Fullness of Time

There are a series of beliefs in existence that directly relate to our individual steps. The most common of which are timing, sequence, significance, and passion/feelings for an action that manipulates its conclusion. Actions that lack any of these qualities will be unsuccessful and will not produce the required results. For example, actions that occur in the wrong sequence or at the wrong time or without the necessary intensity will not produce the desired results. An additional example is certain tropical trees will not survive in a cold climate because all the correct elements are not present. The scriptures put it this way in Galatians chapter 4 verses 4:

> But when the fullness of the time was come, God sent forth his Son made of a women, made under the law.

THE BOOK OF HEBREWS

Prayer from the Bible

And in as much as not without an oath he was made priest: (For those priests were made without an oath; but this with an oath by him that said unto him, The Lord sware and will not repent, Thou art a priest for ever after the order of Melchisedec) By so much was Jesus made a surety of a better testament. And they truly were many priests, because they were not suffered to continue by reason of death: 24 But this man, because he continueth ever, hath an unchangeable priesthood. (Hebrews 7:20-24)

The fullness of time corresponds to the time appointed by the Father, by the law. This is saying that there is a time element involved in everything we do. In essence, be aware of it and don't take shortcuts as this could abort your outcome. Before we concentrate on timing, however, we must correctly identify our patterns. As one continues to scrutinize and study the patterns and outcomes, we should observe how our actions form patterns that help form the person we are becoming. Now consider if they are not the outcomes you were hoping for, you can choose to change your behaviour and actions in order to obtain a different outcome. However, all this begins in the mind with one's thought processes.

Ralph's Speeding Ticket

When we start to distinguish how our actions are repeated, we can benefit from our assessments of them. For example, we can learn to recognize when to take or not take actions based on a previous occurrence of the same performance. That is, if we recognize negative pattern, we can divert its reoccurrence in the future. Here is an experience from real life. My husband, Ralph, would receive a speeding ticket every year around the time of his birthday. This pattern went on for years. He would receive the ticket and then exclaim, "Oh, this is my yearly ticket!" without observing the pattern. However, once he recognized the pattern, he was able to change his thought process so that he no longer anticipated receiving a ticket. This resulted in no speeding traffics tickets at all.

Ralph first had to notice the frequency then assume the traffic ticket was likely to be repeated (based on the pattern) and then take precautions to prevent reoccurrence when his next birthday came around. Now as a result of perceiving the pattern, Ralph has altered the course of his life.

THE BOOK OF HEBREWS

Prayer from the Bible

Wherefore he is able also to save them to the uttermost that come unto God by him, seeing he ever liveth to make intercession for them. For such an high priest became us, who is holy, harmless, undefiled, separate from sinners, and made higher than the heavens; Who needeth not daily, as those high priests, to offer up sacrifice, first for his own sins, and then for the people's: for this he did once, when he offered up himself. For the law maketh men high priests which have infirmity; but the word of the oath, which was since the law, maketh the Son, who is consecrated for evermore. (Hebrews 7:25-28)

CHAPTER 7

Why Are You Here?

Most of us possess a job and a hobby. We often dream of retirement so we can concentrate on our hobby. We use our vacation and spare time to work at our hobbies. Why are we here? One of the reasons we are here is to manifest our passion. Many of us transcend without discovering our true passion. So what is passion? And how does one discover one's passion? Our passion is that special something that we love doing and would do regardless of money, time, or any other obstacle. That hobby oftentimes is our passion. When we operate from our passion, we operate with zeal, excitement, and eagerness. We never get tired or lack enthusiasm. Your passion; that gift, is your love; it is a gift from your Father. One of the insights as to why you are here is the development of your passion.

> But there is a God in heaven (and heaven is within you) who reveals secrets, and He has made know to King Nebuchadnezzar what will be in the latter days. Your dream and the visions of your head upon your bed were these. (Daniel 2: 28)

THE BOOK OF HEBREWS

Prayer from the Bible

Now of the things which we have spoken this is the sum: We have such a high priest, who is set on the right hand of the throne of the Majesty in the heavens; A minister of the sanctuary, and of the true tabernacle, which the Lord pitched, and not man. For every high priest is ordained to offer gifts and sacrifices: wherefore it is of necessity that this man have somewhat also to offer. For if he were on earth, he should not be a priest, seeing that there are priests that offer gifts according to the law: Who serve unto the example and shadow of heavenly things, as Moses was admonished of God when he was about to make the tabernacle: for, See, saith he, that thou make all things according to the pattern shewed to thee in the mount. (Hebrews 8:1-5)

That Inner Speech Is Our Passion

God reveals his secrets. That inner speech from premises of fulfilled desire is the way to create an understandable world for ourselves. That inner speech is our passion. It is our inner conversations, our passion that makes our tomorrows.

Our passion causes us to excel at the very thing we are working on. Passion pushes us to greater heights. We always want to do more, to do better. Our passion gives us purpose. One cannot have passion without purpose. Our passion gives way to our purpose.

> As the deer pants for the water brooks, So pants my soul for you, O God. (Psalm 42: 1)

Spiritual Thirst

The verb "to pant" is expressive of a spiritual thirst. That thirst, that passionate direction, that being on purpose, will make us fulfill our accomplishments. Genuine self-interest means knowing our purpose. In essence, being in agreement with the longings God has written on our heart. It also means pursuing that good that is our existence. We also have a combined purpose, which is to reawaken Christ-like values and steer toward the kingdom of God.

THE BOOK OF HEBREWS

Prayer from the Bible

But now hath he obtained a more excellent ministry, by how much also he is the mediator of a better covenant, which was established upon better promises. For if that first covenant had been faultless, then should no place have been sought for the second. For finding fault with them, he saith, Behold, the days come, saith the Lord, when I will make a new covenant with the house of Israel and with the house of Judah: Not according to the covenant that I made with their fathers in the day when I took them by the hand to lead them out of the land of Egypt; because they continued not in my covenant, and I regarded them not, saith the Lord. (Hebrews 8: 6-9)

Why are we here? We know that we were created in the image and likeness of God. And as such we are spirit, and our body is the temple of the Holy Ghost. If we are spirit created in the image and likeness of God, our function on this planet Earth, therefore, has to be very significant. Could it be said that our purpose on planet Earth is to express the purpose of the Spirit of God? Also could we say that God puts us here to manifest His plan? Could we say that, this may be the very purpose of our creation? In essence, we may possibly pronounce that we are here to do His will. It is a very humbling and thrilling concept to think that we are here to do the will of the Father. However, it posses another question: how do we know His will? Also, further, how do we know his will for us as individuals? And how do we express the purpose of Spirit in this planet Earth?

> But one thing I do not count myself to have apprehended; but one thing I do, forgetting those things which are behind and reaching forward to those things which are ahead, I press toward the goal for the prize of the upward call of God in Christ Jesus. (Philippians 3:13-14)

We Are Always Creating

It is necessary to have an aim in life. Without an aim, we drift as we are always in a state of being and becoming. As a matter of fact, if we are not growing and becoming; we are dying. In essence, we are always in a creating mode as that is the will of the Father. We are never the same one day to the next. Chapter 10 in the book of John states,

> I have come that they may have life, and that they may have it more abundantly.

THE BOOK OF HEBREWS

Prayer from the Bible

For this is the covenant that I will make with the house of Israel after those days, saith the Lord; I will put my laws into their mind, and write them in their hearts: and I will be to them a God, and they shall be to me a people: And they shall not teach every man his neighbour, and every man his brother, saying, Know the Lord: for all shall know me, from the least to the greatest. For I will be merciful to their unrighteousness, and their sins and their iniquities will I remember no more. In that he saith, A new covenant, he hath made the first old. Now that which decayeth and waxeth old is ready to vanish away. (Hebrews 8:10-13)

Abundant life includes salvation, nourishment, healing, and much more. Through the power of our mind, we can have the abundant life Christ promised us.

We can recognize that abundance as it often disguises itself as our passion, that special something we love to do. We must prepare to receive this abundance. If we are serious about receiving abundance, then our first step must be to gradually eliminate all unnecessary thoughts, desires, and habits from our lives. To receive the abundance promised to us, we are obliged to walk in a state of awareness that is awareness of the god that dwells within us. Walking in a state of awareness means to be guided from the inside. It also denotes being still and allowing the Spirit to channel from within. We are the light of the world by which those thoughts that we have sanctioned are made manifest.

> But all things that are exposed are made manifest by the light, for whatever makes manifest is light. (Ephesians 5:13)

THE BOOK OF HEBREWS

Prayer from the Bible

Then verily the first covenant had also ordinances of divine service, and a worldly sanctuary. For there was a tabernacle made; the first, wherein was the candlestick, and the table, and the shewbread; which is called the sanctuary. And after the second veil, the tabernacle which is called the Holiest of all; Which had the golden censer, and the ark of the covenant overlaid round about with gold, wherein was the golden pot that had manna, and Aaron's rod that budded, and the tables of the covenant; And over it the cherubims of glory shadowing the mercyseat; of which we cannot now speak particularly. (Hebrews 9:1-5)

We Are Never Trapped

It is important to remember that as humans, we are in a continuous state of being and becoming. We need to pause and feel the joy and freedom in the fact that we are continually changing day by day. We are never trapped or stuck in any situation regardless of how it might look. Change is always there, waiting for us to make the decision. Knowing that we are in a constant mode of change speaks to why we are here. We are creators. We are creating the world we live in. The creativeness in us comes from our creator. This creativity is guided by the power within. In essence, we are cocreators with our Father. John 15:4 states, "Abide in me, and I in you. As the branch cannot bear fruit of itself." For the branch to produce more fruit, it must abide, which means to dwell, to stay, to settle in, to sink deeper within.

THE BOOK OF HEBREWS

Prayer from the Bible

Now when these things were thus ordained, the priests went always into the first tabernacle, accomplishing the service of God. But into the second went the high priest alone once every year, not without blood, which he offered for himself, and for the errors of the people: The Holy Ghost this signifying, that the way into the holiest of all was not yet made manifest, while as the first tabernacle was yet standing. (Hebrews 9:6-8)

CHAPTER 8

Chances Are We May Have a Habit or Two to Transform, and Then What?

As we survey and examine who we are and try to determine why we are here, chances are we may discover that we have a habit or two to transform. It is evident, therefore, that in order to become the person we know we are in Christ, some change must occur. We therefore must unlearn certain things and replace them with new and exciting patterns and behaviors that will lead us in the direction of becoming our true self. How do we learn these new behaviours? In this concluding chapter, that is the subject for discussion. The main objective is to explain the principles of adult learning and apply them during our quest for knowledge. Understanding how we learn as adults will place us in a position to recognize habits before they are formed into patterns. It will also give us some techniques for implementing planned behaviour, and patterns that will lead to positive outcomes.

> But be ye transformed by the renewing of your mind, that ye may prove what is good, and acceptable, and perfect, will of God. (Romans 12:2)

THE BOOK OF HEBREWS

Prayer from the Bible

But Christ being come an high priest of good things to come, by a greater and more perfect tabernacle, not made with hands, that is to say, not of this building; Neither by the blood of goats and calves, but by his own blood he entered in once into the holy place, having obtained eternal redemption for us. (Hebrews 9:11-12)

Learning Occurs First from Within

Here the scriptures are telling us that change must first occur in the mind before we can make it happen in our day-to-day experiences. Adult learning occurs within each individual as a continual process throughout our lives, and learning also occurs at different speeds among us. So what is learning? Learning is a gaining of knowledge.

That knowledge can either benefit us or harm us. We are bombarded with information every day. We retain some of it and leave the rest behind. So what happens that causes us to retain some information and not others? First, it is important for us to recognize what form of learning will helps us remember pertinent information most effectively. In order to accomplish this, let's look at the average retention rate after twenty-four hours of exposure to new data, and how it can help us in becoming that person we know within.

> Therefore I say to you, whatever things you ask when you pray, believe
> that you receive them, and you will have them. (Mark 11:24)

The emphases on this word is *simply believe*, believing in our inner strength as we press forward.

Lectures—Five Percent Retention

In our search to comprehend who we are, we may attend lectures on self-realization at which we may receive very good information. However, research tells us we will retain only 5 percent of the information received from lectures. It is important to realize that attending one lecture on a subject will not change a well-developed habit. Next, we may obtain several books on various subjects that will enlighten us and help us along our path. In order to implement information gained from books, we must retain it.

THE BOOK OF HEBREWS

Prayer from the Bible

For if the blood of bulls and of goats, and the ashes of an heifer sprinkling the unclean, sanctifieth to the purifying of the flesh: How much more shall the blood of Christ, who through the eternal Spirit offered himself without spot to God, purge your conscience from dead works to serve the living God? (Hebrews 9:13-14)

Reading—10 Percent Retention

It is said that reading allows us to retain just 10 percent of what was comprehended. Here we see the use of lectures plus reading will strengthen our average retention rate. This is clearly telling us that we will retain more when we read and listen to lectures. We also see in order to guard our mind and thoughts, attention must be paid to our listening and reading materials.

Choose for yourselves this day whom you will serve. (Joshua 24:15)

The scriptures are telling us to take a stand. As leaders we must be willing to move ahead and commit to the truth regardless of other people's inclinations.

Sight and Audio—20 Percent Retention

Next on this spectrum is audiovisual. It uses both visual and audio communications that increases our retention average rate to 20 percent. By purchasing an audiovisual tape on the subject matter that will facilitate our change, the likelihood of retention is greater when combined with lecture and reading. In conjunction with audiovisual material, we must pay attention to who is speaking in our ear. Negative thoughts from people speaking in our ear can damage all our good works. Everyone has an opinion and often that opinion may not be the truth of us. It is therefore incumbent upon us to carefully guard our ear by discerning what we open ourselves and mind to.

Whatever things are true, whatever things are noble, whatever things are just, whatever things are pure, whatever things are lovely, whatever things are of good report . . . meditate on these things. (Philippians 4:8)

THE BOOK OF HEBREWS

Prayer from the Bible

And for this cause he is the mediator of the new testament, that by means of death, for the redemption of the transgressions that were under the first testament, they which are called might receive the promise of eternal inheritance. For where a testament is, there must also of necessity be the death of the testator. For a testament is of force after men are dead: otherwise it is of no strength at all while the testator liveth. Whereupon neither the first testament was dedicated without blood. (Hebrews 9:15-18)

Hands-on Approach—30 Percent Retention

The next principle by which adults learn is demonstration. A hands-on approach increases the probability for retention to 30 percent. Sometimes we may find ourselves in a profession that conflicts with our core values. In such cases it is necessary to find another course of employment. Our profession is an extension of us. We made those choices, and they can be changed. It is foolhardy to think that our professional life is distinct and separate from the person we are. We are what we do all day long. What we demonstrate we will retain and become. In other words, if we do it long enough, we will become it.

Our profession must therefore be in alignment with our core values. The scriptures puts it this way: a house divided among itself shall not stand.

Every kingdom divided against itself is brought to desolation; and every city or house divided against itself shall not stand. (Matthew 12:25)

Discussion Groups—50 Percent Retention

A discussion group is also a means by which we learn, and here we retain 50 percent of the information discussed in a group. This is significant as it is telling us that we cannot afford to bash anybody. For if we do, we will retain the garbage we spit out. That garbage then becomes a part of us. We are our thoughts. This means we no longer have the luxury of partaking in the office negative gossip or any negative gossip for that matter. This also speaks to who is speaking in our ear. We must learn to walk away from negative jokes, negative chatter, and negative thoughts on a whole. If we are to take it one step further, one could say we have a responsibility to create positive vibrations.

THE BOOK OF HEBREWS

Prayer from the Bible

For when Moses had spoken every precept to all the people according to the law, he took the blood of calves and of goats, with water, and scarlet wool, and hyssop, and sprinkled both the book, and all the people, Saying, This is the blood of the testament which God hath enjoined unto you. Moreover he sprinkled with blood both the tabernacle, and all the vessels of the ministry. And almost all things are by the law purged with blood; and without shedding of blood is no remission. (Hebrews 9:19-22)

Practice—75 Percent Retention

We have often heard the saying "Practice what you preach." Practice is the next principle by which adults learn. Through practice adults retain 75 percent of information. In an effort to guard our mind and thoughts, we must give consideration to what we are practicing, for it is that we preserve.

Knowing that we retain 75 percent of information when we practice by doing is very significant as this can be the very medium through which new habits can be formed. This also tells us that if we wish to adopt or learn something quickly, we should practice it.

Teaching—90 Percent Retention

The last and most significant way to retaining information is to teach others. The immediate use of new information allows for 90 percent retention of information discussed. This is just awesome. In order to change old habits into new ones, we must teach it to someone else. Teaching others puts us on the fast track to learning and retaining that information. This simply tells me that if I want to learn something fast, teach it to someone. By doing so, I retain 90 percent of the information delivered. Understanding the average rate of retention is important. However, it is also important to be aware of some of the characteristics we possess as adult learners.

THE BOOK OF HEBREWS

Prayer from the Bible

It was therefore necessary that the patterns of things in the heavens should be purified with these; but the heavenly things themselves with better sacrifices than these. For Christ is not entered into the holy places made with hands, which are the figures of the true; but into heaven itself, now to appear in the presence of God for us: Nor yet that he should offer himself often, as the high priest entereth into the holy place every year with blood of others; For then must he often have suffered since the foundation of the world: but now once in the end of the world hath he appeared to put away sin by the sacrifice of himself. (Hebrews 9:23-26)

Characteristics of Adult Learners

Adults tend to be problem centered rather than subject oriented. Our children are subject oriented as they lack our experiences. However, by knowing this, we can conduct inner analyses, define the problem from within, and then implement a course of action to fix it. We are also inclined to be results oriented. Adults do not waste time. We tend to be focused and goal oriented. While our children are future oriented, we are focused on the results that can be achieved in the present.

By understanding this characteristic about ourselves, we will better recognize the effects that can make an impression and be more discerning with regard to the information we allow to take root. Also, we are self-directed. The "teach me" behaviour one often sees in adults could stem from previous school experiences. Generally, adults are independent self-directed learners. Understanding how best we learn can guide us to the best medium when gathering information for change. Mature adults are less trusting and as a result are often skeptical about receiving new information. This is in direct opposition when compared to children who tend to be more accepting. This is a critical point to observe as it speaks to how we learn.

Understanding Our Skepticism

By understanding our skepticism about new information, we can then make a concerted effort to be more open to new ideas and concepts. Coupled with this is another characteristic that suggests that adults seek relevancy. The information we seek must apply to us in the present. Whereas our children are often trained for an unclear future, adults seek the exact information for the situation at hand. The reason for this is as fully developed mature adults, we are internally rather than externally motivated to learn.

THE BOOK OF HEBREWS

Prayer from the Bible

And as it is appointed unto men once to die, but after this the judgment:
So Christ was once offered to bear the sins of many; and unto them that
look for him shall he appear the second time without sin unto salvation.
(Hebrews 9: 27-28)

A word of caution: Because the timing of our learning is related to the issues or concerns developing in our present lives, it is doubly important that we discern the correct information. Time must be taken to seek correct information in order to gain right thinking.

Accepting Responsibility

The majority of us accept responsibility for own learning. This is yet another very important characteristic on how adults learn. If we do not find the correct method of delivery while the information may be worthwhile, it will not be absorbed. It is also important that we find new and efficient ways of learning, one of the main reasons being we have too little time on hand. As adults we must become active participants in the learning process. As a result this means we must become actively involved in the whole process. Anything other than active participation would result in the process having to be repeated several times over.

Previous Knowledge Helps to Shape New

Another point that should not be overlooked is that adults actively create their knowledge. By that, I mean their previous knowledge helps to shape new knowledge. We ascertain what we already know about a topic. In essence, we activate prior knowledge, then personalize it and then elaborate on what we already know. In an effort to determine the truth of us, some housekeeping may be necessary.

THE BOOK OF HEBREWS

Prayer from the Bible

For the law having a shadow of good things to come, and not the very image of the things, can never with those sacrifices which they offered year by year continually make the comers thereunto perfect. For then would they not have ceased to be offered? because that the worshippers once purged should have had no more conscience of sins. (Hebrews 10:1-2)

It may be essential to unlearn some things and take in all new information. This is the most troublesome area we will encounter as the most important factor influencing us is what we have already learned. Adult education is designed to connect with what the learners already know. In this case, however, the effort is to unlearn what is already learned. Knowledge is not passively received; as learners we have to do something with the information; otherwise, it will not result in long-term retention.

Barriers Stem from Negative Thinking

As adults we stumble upon many barriers to learning. These barriers stem from years of negative thinking that we encountered throughout our lives. Some of the barriers we bring to learning may be low self-esteem, anxiety, fear, and insecurity. Fear and frustration are the most problematic as they often lead to hopelessness that stunt our learning. We also possess an unwillingness to ask for help, which also stems from fear. Coupled with the low self-esteem is a lack of confidence and low expectations of ourselves. On top of all that, we may also bring to the learning table our domestic, financial, or personal worries, and to top it off any health conditions we are nursing at the time.

Hopefully, by discovering who we are from the earlier chapters in the book, some of these barriers we would leave behind. The barriers we bring to the learning table can be viewed as emotions. This is not as bad as it may appear as emotions are the key to learning. As we go through this whole process of unlearning and learning information, it is important to understand how our brain processes learned material. Information is stored in the mind as a network of multiple interconnected and related data. As a result, the processing of our thoughts leads to the activation of other related material. We have already discussed that the use of images can aid the learning process and retention, better than verbal description.

THE BOOK OF HEBREWS

Prayer from the Bible

But in those sacrifices there is a remembrance again made of sins every year. For it is not possible that the blood of bulls and of goats should take away sins. Wherefore when he cometh into the world, he saith, Sacrifice and offering thou wouldest not, but a body hast thou prepared me. (Hebrews 10:3-5)

Adults Are Problem Solvers

As adults, we are all about problem solving. We must also have a view of the big picture. We operate better from the end result. In other words, we know where we want to end up first, and then we set a course of action. We may understand our end result; however, attracting it through our thought process is quite another matter. As adults we learn not primarily by receiving and copying impressions and information, but rather by assembling and reassembling our own mental formation of our world. In other words, understanding is largely internally constructed. Our brain is a complex organ, and correct thinking requires deep processing. For correct thinking to become a part of who we are, the information must be obtained through self-directed learning. In essence, learning must be within our control. We must be able to accept responsibility for our own learning. Having said that, it is important to remember that our judgments of our own ability are central to our actions.

We should note that on a number of occasions our self-judgments may not be accurate. In such instances, verbal persuasion from a credible source could prove valuable.

Chinese Proverb

The Master Prophet often states that writing is the first form of manifestation. Writing also plays an important role in an adult learning principle called insightful observance. This insightful observance of thinking back will help shape and correct actions that may affect future practice. Writing can provide the vehicle for these insightful observances. Finally, I would like to end with this Chinese proverb that states, "Tell me and I'll forget, show me and I may remember, involve me and I'll understand."

THE BOOK OF HEBREWS

Prayer from the Bible

In burnt offerings and sacrifices for sin thou hast had no pleasure. Then said I, Lo, I come (in the volume of the book it is written of me,) to do thy will, O God. (Hebrews 10:6-7)

GLOSSARY OF TERMS

astral body. The astral body refers to the concept of a subtle body that exists alongside the physical body as a vehicle of the soul or consciousness. It is usually understood as being of an emotional nature and, as such, it is equated to the desire body or emotional body.

Bible. The word "Bible" refers to the canonical collections of sacred writings or books of Judaism and Christianity. Books included as canon in the Bible vary according to different traditions. Judaism's Bible, often referred to as the Hebrew Bible or Tanakh, includes the books common to both the Christian and Jewish biblical canons. Its most sacred part, the Torah, is traditionally considered by believers to be God's direct words and is the origin of much of Jewish religious law.

The Christian Bible is often called the Holy Bible, scriptures, or word of God. It divides the books of the Bible into two parts: the Old Testament primarily sourced from the Tanakh (with some variations), and the New Testament containing books originally written primarily in Greek. Some versions of the Christian Bible have a separate Apocrypha section for the books not considered part of the Christian biblical canon according to that version. Additional versions exist, such as the Roman Catholic and Eastern Orthodox Old Testament canons, which contain books not found in the Tanakh but that are found in the Greek Septuagint, the oldest of several ancient translations of the Hebrew Bible into Greek.

THE BOOK OF HEBREWS

Prayer from the Bible

Above when he said, Sacrifi ce and offering and burnt offerings and offering for sin thou wouldest not, neither hadst pleasure therein; which are offered by the law; Then said he, Lo, I come to do thy will, O God. He taketh away the fi rst, that he may establish the second. (Hebrews 10:8-9)

body. With regard to living things, a body is the integral physical material of an individual. In the views emerging from the mind-body dichotomy, the body is considered in contrasts with mind/soul/personality/behavior and therefore considered as little valued *http://en.wikipedia.org/wiki/Body-note-Young* and trivial. Many modern philosophers of mind maintain that the mind is not something separate from the body

clairvoyance. From seventeenth century French *clair*, meaning "clear" and *voyant* meaning "seeing," this is a term used to describe the purported transference of information about an object, location, or physical event through means other than the five traditional senses. A person said to have this ability is referred to as a clairvoyant.

consubstantial. Christ Jesus, coeternal and consubstantial with the Father and with the Holy Ghost. This means "regarded as the same in substance or essence" (as of the three persons of the Trinity).

cosmos. In its most general sense, a cosmos is an orderly or harmonious system. It originates from a Greek term *κόσμος*—meaning "order, orderly arrangement, ornaments"—and is the antithetical concept of chaos. The word "cosmetics" originates from the same root.

Creation. The belief that God brought the universe into existence (theology).

critical thinking. This consists of the mental process of analyzing and evaluating statements or propositions that have been offered as true. It includes a process of reflecting on the specific meaning of statements, examining offered evidence, and reasoning in order to form judgment.

Critical thinkers can gather information from verbal or written expression, reflection, observation, experience, and reasoning. Critical thinking has its basis in intellectual criteria that go beyond subject-matter divisions and which include clarity, credibility, accuracy, precision, relevance, depth, breadth, logic, significance, and fairness.

THE BOOK OF HEBREWS

Prayer from the Bible

By the which will we are sanctified through the offering of the body of Jesus Christ once for all. And every priest standeth daily ministering and offering oftentimes the same sacrifices, which can never take away sins. (Hebrews 10:10-11)

divine economy. From the Greek word *oikonomia* (economy), literally "management of a household" or "stewardship."

It is the elements and resources revealed by God as necessary for salvation through special revelation (scriptures of the Old and New Testament).

The ultimate expression of this in theology would be the work of salvation achieved by Jesus Christ on the cross. His sacrifice paid for our debts and therefore has made payment for our sins—and therefore we are seen as not guilty before God for our sins committed.

This economy is related to a transaction. God gives the means of salvation through Jesus's sacrifice. We accept it through faith and allegiance to Him.

As such, it is an economy as it has resources, management and accountability.

end times. Also called end of days) Usually refers to the eschatological ideas in the three Abrahamic religions (Judaism, Christianity, and Islam). The end times are often (but not always) depicted as a time of tribulation that precede the predicted coming of a messianic figure.

etheric body. The etheric body, ether body, aether body, or vital body is one of the subtle bodies in esoteric philosophies, in some religious teachings. It is understood as a sort of life force body or aura that constitutes the "blue."

manifestations. In the mystical traditions, the manifest, or being, is that which exists.

mental body. The mental body (the mind) is one of the subtle bodies in esoteric philosophies, in some religious teachings. It is understood as a sort of body made up of thoughts, just as the emotional body consists of emotions and the physical body is made up of matter. In occult understanding, thoughts are not just subjective *qualia* but have an existence apart from the associated physical organ, the brain.

THE BOOK OF HEBREWS

Prayer from the Bible

But this man, after he had offered one sacrifice for sins for ever, sat down on the right hand of God; From henceforth expecting till his enemies be made his footstool. (Hebrews 10:12-13)

New Testament. It is a collection of twenty-seven books, produced by Christians, with Jesus as its central figure, written primarily in Koine Greek in the early Christian period. Nearly all Christians recognize the New Testament (as stated below) as canonical scripture. These books can be grouped into:

The Gospels

> ➤ Synoptic Gospels
> ➤ Gospel According to Matthew (Mt)
> ➤ Gospel According to Mark (Mk)
> ➤ Gospel According to Luke (Lk)
> ➤ Gospel According to John (Jn)
> ➤ Acts of the Apostles (Ac; continues Luke)

Pauline Epistles

> ➤ Epistle to the Romans, (Ro)
> ➤ First Epistle to the Corinthians (1Co)
> ➤ Second Epistle to the Corinthians (2Co)
> ➤ Epistle to the Galatians (Ga)
> ➤ Epistle to the Ephesians (Ep)
> ➤ Epistle to the Philippians (Pp)
> ➤ Epistle to the Colossians (Cl)
> ➤ First Epistle to the Thessalonians (1Th)
> ➤ Second Epistle to the Thessalonians (2Th)

Pastoral Epistles

> ➤ First Epistle to Timothy (1Ti)
> ➤ Second Epistle to Timothy (2Ti)
> ➤ Epistle to Titus (Tt)
> ➤ Epistle to Philemon (Pm)
> ➤ Epistle to the Hebrews (He)

THE BOOK OF HEBREWS

Prayers from the Bible

For by one offering he hath perfected for ever them that are sanctified. Whereof the Holy Ghost also is a witness to us: for after that he had said before, This is the covenant that I will make with them after those days, saith the Lord, I will put my laws into their hearts, and in their minds will I write them. And their sins and iniquities will I remember no more. Now where remission of these is, there is no more offering for sin. Having therefore, brethren, boldness to enter into the holiest by the blood of Jesus, By a new and living way, which he hath consecrated for us, through the veil, that is to say, his flesh; And having an high priest over the house of God. (Hebrews 10:14-21)

General Epistles (also called Jewish Epistles)

- ➢ Epistle of James (Jm)
- ➢ First Epistle of Peter (1Pe)
- ➢ Second Epistle of Peter (2Pe)
- ➢ First Epistle of John (1Jn)
- ➢ Second Epistle of John (2Jn)
- ➢ Third Epistle of John (3Jn)
- ➢ Epistle of Jude (Jd; critical thinking)
- ➢ Revelation (Re)

Old Testament. It is the first section of the two-part Christian biblical canon, which includes the books of the Hebrew Bible as well as several deuterocanonical books. Its exact contents differ in the various Christian denominations.

The Protestant Old Testament is, for the most part, identical with the Hebrew Bible. The differences between the Hebrew Bible and the Protestant Old Testament are minor, dealing only with the arrangement and number of the books. For example, while the Hebrew Bible considers Kings to be a unified text, the Protestant Old Testament divides it into two books. Similarly, Ezra and Nehemiah are considered to be one book in the Hebrew Bible.

The differences between the Hebrew Bible and other versions of the Old Testament such as the Samaritan Pentateuch, Syriac, Latin, Greek, and other canons, are greater. Many of these canons include books and even sections of books that the others do not. For a full discussion of these differences, see books of the Bible. An important difference as well can lie in the translations of various words from the original Hebrew.

There is abundant and reliable evidence that these books were written before the birth of Jesus of Nazareth, whose teaching and immediate disciples' deeds and teachings are the subject of the subsequent writings of the Christian New Testament.

The scriptures used by Jesus were according to Luke 24:44-49: "The law of Moses, and in the prophets, and in the psalms . . . the scriptures." According to most Bible scholars, the Old Testament was composed between the fifth century BC and the second century BC though parts of it, such as parts of the Torah and the Song of Deborah (Judges 5), probably date back much earlier.

THE BOOK OF HEBREWS

Prayers of the Bible

Let us draw near with a true heart in full assurance of faith, having our hearts sprinkled from an evil conscience, and our bodies washed with pure water. Let us hold fast the profession of our faith without wavering; (for he is faithful that promised;) And let us consider one another to provoke unto love and to good works: Not forsaking the assembling of ourselves together, as the manner of some is; but exhorting one another: and so much the more, as ye see the day approaching. (Hebrews 10:22-25)

Omega Point. Is a term invented by French Jesuit Pierre Teilhard de Chardin to describe the ultimate maximum level of complexity consciousness, considered by him the aim to be the direction toward which consciousness evolve.

tensile strength. The maximum load that a material can support without fracture when being stretched, divided by the original cross-sectional area of the material.

triadocentric. Considers the divine life ad intra as well as that life ad extra, always beginning with the whole of the Trinity according to the patristic principle: everything proceeds from the Father, through the Son, in the Holy Spirit.

triadophoric. Relating to the Trinity.

Trinity. In Christianity, the doctrine of the Trinity states that God is one being who exists, simultaneously and eternally, as a mutual indwelling of three persons: the Father, the Son (incarnate as Jesus of Nazareth), and the Holy Spirit. Since the fourth century, in both Eastern and Western Christianity, this doctrine has been stated as "three persons in one God," all three of whom, as distinct and coeternal persons, are of one indivisible divine essence, a simple being. Supporting the doctrine of the Trinity is known as Trinitarianism.

Triadic. In logic, mathematics, and semiotics, a triadic relation or a ternary relation is an important special case of a polyadic or finitary relation, one in which the number of places in the relation is three. One also sees the adjectives "3-adic," "3-ary," "3-dim," or "3-place" being used to describe these relations.

Mathematics is positively rife with examples of 3-adic relations, and a sign relation, the archidea of the whole field of semiotics, is a special case of a 3-adic relation.

Source: *Wikipedia* (http://en.wikipedia.org)

THE BOOK OF HEBREWS

Prayer from the Bible

For if we sin wilfully after that we have received the knowledge of the truth, there remaineth no more sacrifice for sins, 27 But a certain fearful looking for of judgment and fiery indignation, which shall devour the adversaries. 28 He that despised Moses' law died without mercy under two or three witnesses: 29 Of how much sorer punishment, suppose ye, shall he be thought worthy, who hath trodden under foot the Son of God, and hath counted the blood of the covenant, wherewith he was sanctified, an unholy thing, and hath done despite unto the Spirit of grace? (Hebrews 10:26-29)

RESOURCES

The following recommended books are among the best of thousands we could consult as we continue our journey. Space does not permit listing the publisher's address for each of the following books; however, one could contact Zoe Ministries for more information on Bishop E. Bernard Jordan Books.

The Achiever's Guide to Success. 1996 by Bishop E. Bernard Jordan
Breaking SOUL Ties and Generational Curses 1993 Dr. E. Bernard Jordan
His Color Was Black A Race Attack 1996 Bishop E. Bernard Jordan
Into The DEPTHS The Company of Prophets Searches The Hidden Mysteries
    of The Prophetic. 2007 by E. Bernard Jordan
The Holy Spirit 1992 Dr. E. Bernard Jordan
The Joshua Generation 1996 Dr. E. Bernard Jordan
Keys To Liberation 1995 Bishop E. Bernard Jordan
The LAWS of Thinking 20 secrets to Using the Divine Power of Your Mind
    to Manifest Prosperity 2006 by E. Bernard Jordan
The Making of The Dream 1991 Bishop E. Bernard Jordan
The Mastery of Mentorship 1995 Bishop E. Bernard Jordan
Meditation A Key to New Horizons in God 1996 E. Bernard Jordan
Mentoring the Missing Link 1989 Bernard Jordan
The Power of Money 1992 Dr. E. Bernard Jordan
Prophetic Genesis 1996 Dr. E. Bernard Jordan
The Science of Prophecy 1996 Dr. E. Bernard Jordan
The Seed of Destiny 1991 Dr. E Bernard Jordan
The Spirit of Liberation 1996 Bishop E. Bernard Jordan
Written Judgments 1989 Prophet Bernard Jordan

MESSAGE TO THE READERS

Taylor-Boyce, cofounder and CEO of Total Gratutidue, has broad-ranging experience working with companies designing, developing, and reengineering workplace training material. A consummate value-driven professional, she is well respected in the field of occupational health and safety. Taylor-Boyce possesses a reputation for driving quantifiable advances to help alleviate the economic burden placed on companies.

This passion, dedication, and concern for human safety and well-being are the impetus behind this new work. Her book is for seekers of truth. It is an aid to those new to the path of faith and truth. Truth can only be understood when we are in a state of mind of attention. As a result, truth is not available to us if our minds are not conditioned to receive it. This book is our conditioner.

Figuratively speaking, truth can only be found at the bottom of a well. And we know a well is a very deep and dark place. This is telling us that truth must be sought after and come upon with earnest effort. Also, we must dig deep in pursuit of truth. This book will prepare our mind for that truth that we seek.

There are a series of beliefs in existence that directly relate to our individual steps. The most common of which are timing, sequence, significance, and passion/feelings for an action that manipulates its conclusion. Actions that lack any of these qualities will be unsuccessful and will not produce the required results.

For example, actions that occur in the wrong sequence or at the wrong time or without the necessary intensity will not produce the desired results. An additional example is that certain tropical trees will not survive in a cold climate because all the correct elements are not present. The scriptures put it this way in Galatians chapter 4 verses 4: "But when the fullness of the time was come, God sent forth his Son made of a women, made under the law."

Finally, we are told that the achievement of wisdom and power can only be acquired through study and knowledge of ourselves. We also know that there are laws governing this universe. Furthermore, we know that the same laws that govern man govern the whole universe. May this book give support to the acquirement of our wisdom.

INDEX

Printed in the United States
123702LV00002B/2/P